Intricate Design Coloring Book One

Mary Ann Seymour

Printed by Create Space, An Amazon.com Company

Available from Amazon.com, Create Space.com and other online stores

Preface

This book is dedicated to my immediate family and to all the people who have encouraged me to press on. It has been a time of great testing, during which I have learned a great deal. Thus, it has also been a time of learning to lean into the Lord and learning to trust Him more fully. I pray that this book will prove to be a blessing in your life and thus extend to all those you love. Enjoy yourself this pleasure. Life passes quickly and we look back and wish that we had spent more time soaking up the pleasures that God has provided for us.

Go on, pick up those colored pencils and color some of these. You know you want to. You know you do! Remember how you used to color when you were younger?

Why you would want to color:

- You want something different to do.
- You like a challenge.
- You love color.
- You loved to color when you were younger.
- Science has proven that coloring is a stress relieving, relaxing therapy.
- It is an activity you can share with your children.
- It is an activity you can do when the electricity is off and there is no TV, or other electronic devices working!
- The worrisome thoughts that you have had will be forgotten as you concentrate on which colors to use and where to us them.

Add some soothing music to that and you have a winning

combination.

You will find some pictures quite easy to color. Others will be a real challenge. I wanted to try something different, so I added some that have added shading. Some have dark lines and light lines. If coloring the smaller sections with the light lines is too much of a challenge, just color over them. Don't feel as though you must color ever space. I think they look nice with some white spaces.

I believe that you will enjoy this book. I hope so. I have enjoyed making the designs. Putting it together was not the part I enjoyed most. I just wanted to keep making more designs. So, I decided to make book two. It will soon follow this one.

May your joy be full as you color the pages in this book.

About the Designer

Mary Ann does not claim to be an artist, but she says that, if, given a pencil, an eraser as long as a pencil, as well as a picture to look at, she can at times, draw something that looks, just a little like the original. However, she does like to doodle, and from that developed the ability to make coloring designs. She also likes to use software to produce beautiful fractal designs which she prints out and frames, and/or shrinks and puts into jewelry. She also likes to make colored kaleidoscope designs and kaleidoscope designs that move. She hopes to soon have some of these products for sale on line. Intricate Coloring Book Two will soon be on its way. Look for it. Blessings to all.

www.ingramcontent.com/pod-product-compliance
Lightning Source LLC
Chambersburg PA
CBHW081219280526
45787CB00006B/2447